A TRUE BOOK™

DIGGING IN GEOLOGY

All About Rocks

Discovering the World Beneath Your Feet

Alessandra Potenza

Children's Press®
An Imprint of Scholastic Inc.

Content Consultant
Dr. Wen-lu Zhu
Professor of Geology
Department of Geology
University of Maryland, College Park

Library of Congress Cataloging-in-Publication Data

Names: Potenza, Alessandra, author.

Title: All about rocks: discovering the world beneath your feet / Alessandra Potenza.

Other titles: All about rocks

Description: New York: Children's Press, an imprint of Scholastic Inc., 2021. | Series: A true book | Includes index. | Audience: Ages 8-10. | Audience: Grades 4-6. | Summary: "This book introduces readers to rocks"— Provided by publisher.

Identifiers: LCCN 2020035267 | ISBN 9780531137147 (paperback) | ISBN 9780531137109 (library binding)

Subjects: LCSH: Rocks—Juvenile literature. | Petrology—Juvenile literature.

Classification: LCC QE432.2 .P68 2021 | DDC 552—dc23

LC record available at https://lccn.loc.gov/2020035267

Design by Kathleen Petelinsek
Editorial development by Priyanka Lamichhane

Scholastic Inc., 557 Broadway, New York, NY 10012

1 2 3 4 5 6 7 8 9 10 R 30 29 28 27 26 25 24 23 22 21

Front cover: Background and center right photos: sandstone; top right: marble; bottom left: basalt rock columns

Back cover: A volcanologist wears protective gear while taking a sample of lava.

Find the Truth!

Everything you are about to read is true *except* for one of the sentences on this page.

Which one is **TRUE**?

T or F The oldest rocks on Earth are 10 billion years old.

T or F Earth's crust is made up of the continents and ocean floor.

Find the answers in this book.

What's in This Book?

The **BIG** Truth

An asteroid

Are There Rocks Flying Around in Space?

Sedimentary rock

To learn about the tools scientists use to study rocks, turn to page 36!

Dig In!

Today, the Grand Canyon in Arizona is a **breathtaking landscape** that stretches farther than the eye can see. For long periods of time, the land looked **completely different**: It was covered in sand dunes, similar to those you see in a desert. At other times, it was covered by a shallow sea.

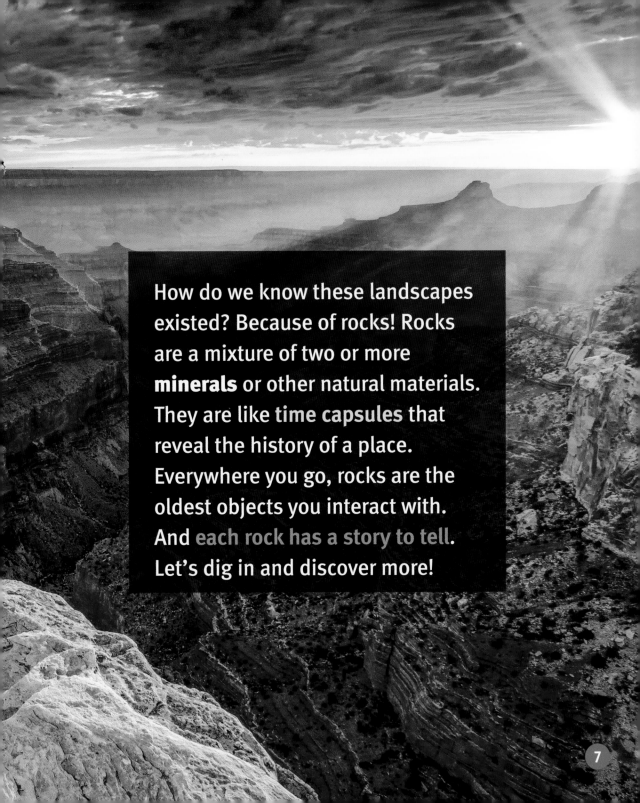

How do we know these landscapes existed? Because of rocks! Rocks are a mixture of two or more **minerals** or other natural materials. They are like time capsules that reveal the history of a place. Everywhere you go, rocks are the oldest objects you interact with. And each rock has a story to tell. Let's dig in and discover more!

Earth is a rocky planet, but more than 70 percent of its surface is covered by ocean.

Rocks make Earth's continents—and also the bottom of the sea.

Our Rocky Planet

Look outside your window. Do you see pebbles scattered on the ground? Hilltops in the distance? Maybe a stone building across the street? You're looking at rocks. From tiny stones to towering mountains, rocks are all around us. In fact, without them, our planet wouldn't exist. Earth is almost entirely made up of rocks. But where did all these rocks come from?

Earth's Birth

Earth is one of eight planets that orbit the sun. These planets formed about 4.6 billion years ago, when a giant cloud of dust and gas began swirling around the sun. The dust and gas started clumping together. Rocky materials that could withstand the sun's scorching heat formed the four rocky planets of our solar system, including Earth. Farther out, gas and ice lumped together into four more planets.

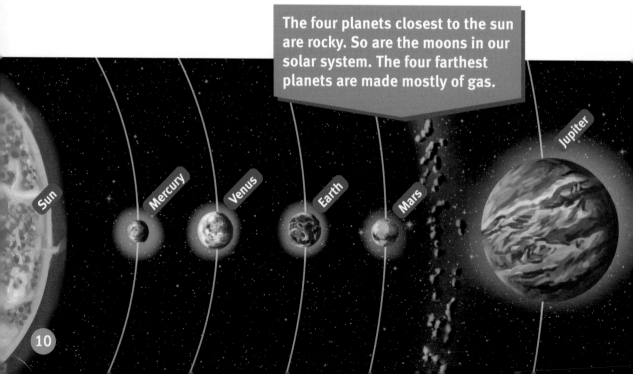

The four planets closest to the sun are rocky. So are the moons in our solar system. The four farthest planets are made mostly of gas.

Sun

Mercury

Venus

Earth

Mars

Jupiter

Fiery Mess

When you were a baby, you probably looked very different than you do today. The same is true of Earth. In the beginning, our planet was incredibly hot. It was so hot that there was no solid surface. Earth was just a big ball of molten rock. After several hundred million years, the planet began to cool. Earth's surface solidified into a rocky crust. The very first solid rocks were formed.

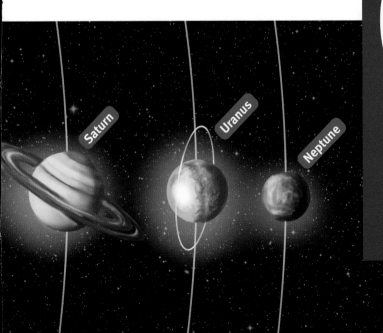

Early Earth was a ball of scorching hot molten rock, with no solid surface.

Saturn

Uranus

Neptune

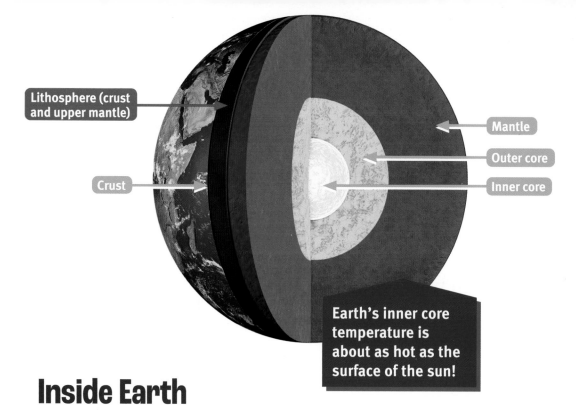

Lithosphere (crust and upper mantle)

Crust

Mantle

Outer core

Inner core

Earth's inner core temperature is about as hot as the surface of the sun!

Inside Earth

Earth is like an egg: It's divided into layers. Earth's crust is the eggshell. It's made up of the continents and the ocean floor, both made of rocks. Below the crust is Earth's mantle—the egg white. The mantle is made mostly of solid rocks. But some regions are so hot that the rocks are partially melted. Earth's core—the egg yolk—is made of two parts. The outer core is made up of liquid metals. The inner core is made of iron and nickel.

Building Blocks

Look closely at a rock and you'll notice chunks and streaks of different colors and sizes. These are the minerals that make up the rock. There are more than 5,000 minerals on Earth. But about 90 percent of the rocks in Earth's crust are made of just one group of minerals: silicates. Silicates include the most abundant **elements** found in the crust: oxygen and silicon. These elements were created inside stars!

Feldspar (mineral)

Quartz (mineral)

Granite (rock)

This rock, called granite, is made up of different minerals, including quartz and feldspar. Quartz and feldspar are the most common silicate minerals in Earth's crust.

Rocks are different colors because of the minerals they contain.

Rocks come in colorful varieties. Have you ever seen any rocks that look like these?

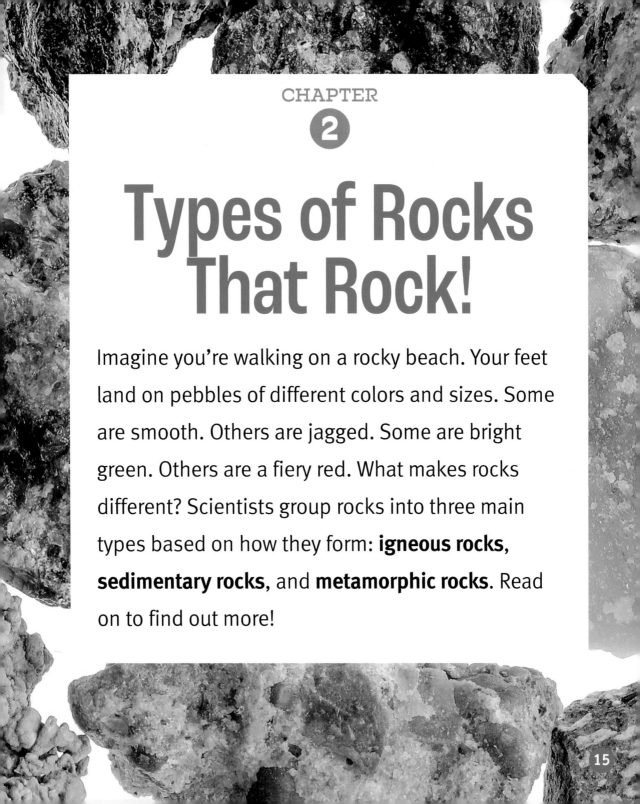

Types of Rocks That Rock!

Imagine you're walking on a rocky beach. Your feet land on pebbles of different colors and sizes. Some are smooth. Others are jagged. Some are bright green. Others are a fiery red. What makes rocks different? Scientists group rocks into three main types based on how they form: **igneous rocks**, **sedimentary rocks**, and **metamorphic rocks**. Read on to find out more!

Igneous Rocks

Earth's mantle and crust contain chambers of hot, melted rock known as magma. When a volcano erupts, magma shoots out as lava. As the lava quickly cools and hardens, it forms igneous rocks. Magma that hardens on the surface forms what's called extrusive igneous rock. This includes basalt and pumice. Sometimes magma cools slowly and hardens underground, surrounded by other rocks. This process forms intrusive igneous rock, such as granite.

Pumice can float. How? It's filled with air bubbles!

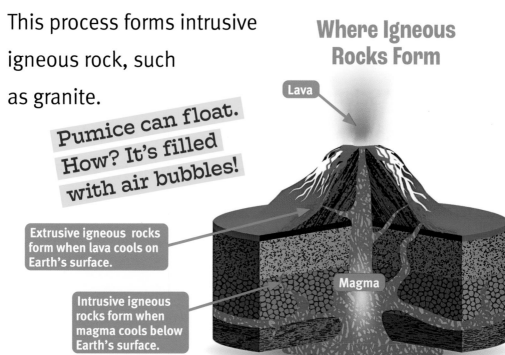

Where Igneous Rocks Form

Lava

Magma

Extrusive igneous rocks form when lava cools on Earth's surface.

Intrusive igneous rocks form when magma cools below Earth's surface.

The rough texture of granite, an intrusive igneous rock, is seen on this mountaintop in the Sierra Nevada mountains of California.

In Rome, Italy, cobblestones called *sanpietrini* are made of the extrusive igneous rock basalt.

Basalt

The word "igneous" comes from *ignis*, the Latin word for fire.

Smooth or Rough?

When magma reaches the surface, it cools quickly—within days, hours, or even minutes. This leaves little time for minerals in the magma to grow. As a result, extrusive igneous rocks usually have a smooth texture. When magma cools below the surface, it does so slowly—taking thousands to millions of years. This allows mineral grains to grow large. As a result, intrusive igneous rocks usually have a rough texture.

Sedimentary Rocks

Sedimentary rocks are made from sediment—bits of rocks, sand, and even the shells of small marine animals. Wind and water move sediment around Earth's surface. When sediment settles into one place, it piles up in flat layers. Over thousands or even millions of years, these layers are buried and pressed together. Then the layers harden into rock.

How Sedimentary Rocks Form

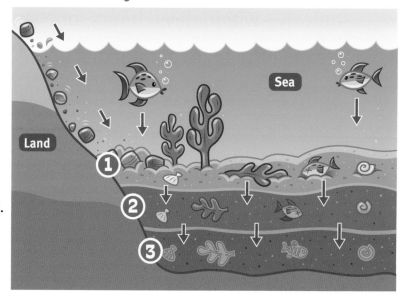

1 Sediment such as sand and seashells settles at the bottom of the sea in flat layers.

2 The layers of sediment are buried and pressed together under more sediment.

3 The bottom layers of sediment turn to rock over a very long period of time.

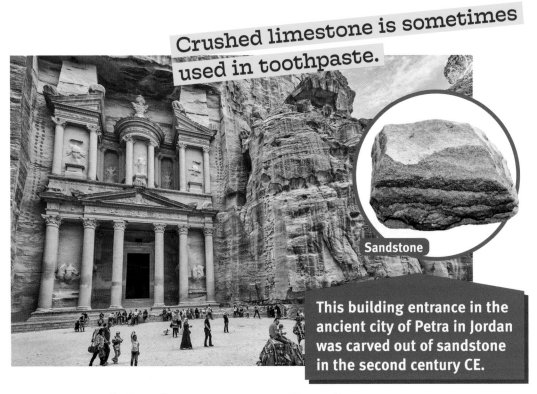

Crushed limestone is sometimes used in toothpaste.

Sandstone

This building entrance in the ancient city of Petra in Jordan was carved out of sandstone in the second century CE.

Types of Sedimentary Rocks

Different types of sediment form different types of sedimentary rocks. For example, layers of sand that get buried and pressed over time form sandstone. You can often see those original layers of sand in the sandstone itself. Limestone is another type of sedimentary rock. It is made from the skeletons of ancient marine animals, such as corals, that piled up underwater.

Metamorphic Rocks

Sometimes rocks that were on Earth's surface are dragged deep underground. There, extreme heat and pressure squeeze the rocks. The minerals in rocks react with each other and with fluids inside Earth, forming new minerals. This process turns the original rocks into metamorphic rocks. They now look different and have new properties. Any rock can become a metamorphic rock!

How Metamorphic Rocks Form

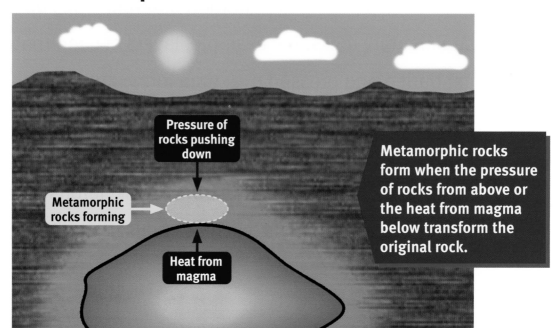

Pressure of rocks pushing down

Metamorphic rocks forming

Heat from magma

Metamorphic rocks form when the pressure of rocks from above or the heat from magma below transform the original rock.

Between 1501 and 1504, Italian artist Michelangelo made *David*, one of the world's most famous statues, out of marble.

Marble

"Marble" comes from the Greek word *marmar*, which means "to shine."

Types of Metamorphic Rocks

Marble is a well-known metamorphic rock. It has been used since ancient times to make statues and buildings. Marble comes from the sedimentary rock limestone. Extreme heat and pressure squeeze limestone into hard marble. Gneiss (pronounced nice) is another type of metamorphic rock. It comes from igneous or sedimentary rocks. During the transformation of granite into gneiss, the minerals in granite are put under so much pressure that they separate into layers.

Are There Rocks Flying Around in Space?

Yes! Space not only has rocky planets and moons. It is also filled with other rocks such as zooming comets, asteroids, and meteoroids. Many of these rocky structures orbit our sun. If these space rocks come close to Earth during their trip around our star, they are called Near-Earth Objects. Let's take a closer look!

More than 3,600 known comets are in our solar system.

Comets: Dusty Snowballs

Comets are balls of rock, ice, gases, and dust. Each comet has a heart of ice called a nucleus. When a comet gets close to the sun, some of the ice evaporates, or turns from liquid into gas. Gas and dust create a tail that can stretch for millions of miles.

Asteroids: Planet Busters

Asteroids come in many shapes and sizes. Some are made of small rocks loosely grouped together. Others are huge chunks of rock that are as big as cities. There are asteroids so large that they have moons circling around them. If a big asteroid were to hit our planet, it would create major damage!

Meteoroids: Rocky Fireballs

Meteoroids are small chunks of rock that usually come from asteroids or comets. Meteoroids that burn up completely when they pass through Earth's atmosphere are called meteors. They create a streak of light we usually call a shooting star. Some meteoroids land on Earth. These are called meteorites.

There are about 1,500 active volcanoes around the world.

Lava spews into the air from the Bardarbunga volcano in Iceland.

Rocks on the Move

The oldest known rocks on Earth are about 4 billion years old. That's almost as old as Earth itself. But most rocks are younger, and new rocks are forming all the time. This is because our planet is an ever-changing and active place. Rocks are constantly forming, breaking, and bonding through natural processes. Older rocks are constantly transformed into new rocks.

Earth's Power Tools

You may think that nothing can destroy rocks. But over time, they wear away and break apart. This process is called **weathering,** and it is caused by water, wind, and **gravity**—Earth's very own power tools. Water can seep into cracks in a rock and expand as it freezes, splitting the rock. Wind can carry debris that wears away at a rock. Sometimes plants are to blame. If plant roots grow inside cracks in a rock, the rock can crumble.

Timeline: Uses of Rocks Through History

3.3 MILLION YEARS AGO
Early human ancestors in present-day Africa began using tools made of rocks.

800,000 YEARS AGO
Early humans use rocks called flint to make sparks and start fires.

2000 TO 1200 BCE
Ancient Egyptians use minerals like galena, found in igneous and metamorphic rocks, to produce black eye makeup.

80 CE
Ancient Romans finish building the Colosseum using concrete, a mixture made with limestone and volcanic ash.

Moving Around

When rocks are broken apart, the pieces don't just stay where they are. Wind and water carry the pieces—or sediments—to other places. This process is called **erosion**. The sediments then settle and create other landforms, such as beaches and islands. The settling of sediments is called **deposition**. Weathering, erosion, and deposition break down rocks and move them all over Earth's surface. These processes happen over thousands or even millions of years.

1621
North America's first gristmill, which typically uses granite and sandstone to grind grain, is built in Jamestown, Virginia.

1795
A French scientist named Nicolas-Jacques Conté invents the modern pencil by mixing clay and the mineral graphite, found in igneous and metamorphic rocks, to place in the pencil.

1800
James Pillans, a geography teacher in Scotland, is among the first to build a chalkboard using the metamorphic rock slate.

TODAY
Rocks are used to make countertops, tiles, concrete, and other home and construction materials.

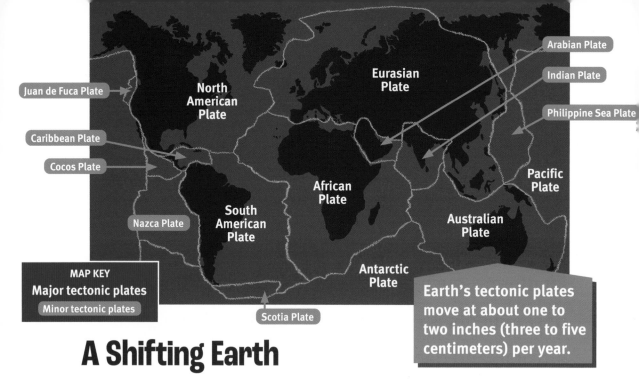

Juan de Fuca Plate

Caribbean Plate

Cocos Plate

North American Plate

Nazca Plate

South American Plate

African Plate

Eurasian Plate

Arabian Plate

Indian Plate

Philippine Sea Plate

Pacific Plate

Australian Plate

Antarctic Plate

Scotia Plate

MAP KEY
Major tectonic plates
Minor tectonic plates

Earth's tectonic plates move at about one to two inches (three to five centimeters) per year.

A Shifting Earth

Rocks aren't just moved around Earth's surface. They are also pushed down into the mantle. How does this happen? Earth's surface is like a jigsaw puzzle. The lithosphere is divided into slabs of rock called **tectonic plates**. These plates are constantly shifting. When they push against each other or one plate slides under another, rocks in Earth's lithosphere can be dragged deep inside the planet. There, they can turn into igneous rocks if melted or they can transform into metamorphic rocks.

Boom and Shake!

Tectonic plates move at about the same rate that your fingernails grow. These movements can unleash powerful events. When one plate slides under another plate or when they move away from each other, magma can shoot up to the surface, resulting in a volcanic eruption. As tectonic plates move along faults, or cracks in Earth's crust, stress can build up. When that stress is released, the ground shakes, resulting in an earthquake.

About 20,000 earthquakes happen around the world every year.

In 2018, a powerful earthquake in Anchorage, Alaska, caused major damage to roads.

A Never-Ending Cycle

The processes of weathering, erosion, and tectonic plate movements are the engines behind the rock cycle. The cycle is the endless journey of rocks moving from Earth's surface to its interior and back up again, while changing from one type of rock to another. This happens over the course of millions of years. Old rocks are constantly transformed into new rocks.

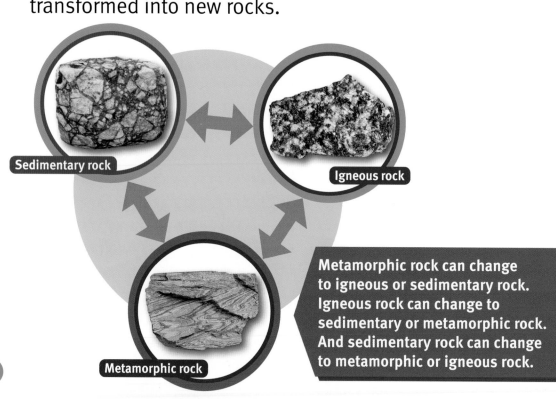

Sedimentary rock

Igneous rock

Metamorphic rock

Metamorphic rock can change to igneous or sedimentary rock. Igneous rock can change to sedimentary or metamorphic rock. And sedimentary rock can change to metamorphic or igneous rock.

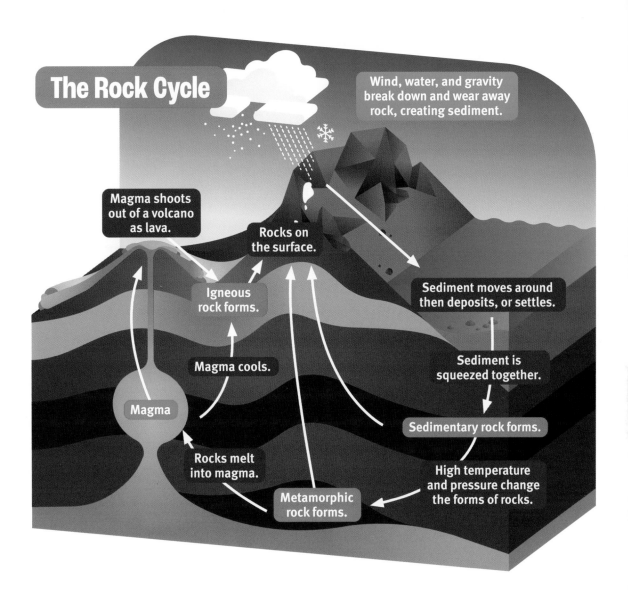

The Rock Cycle

Wind, water, and gravity break down and wear away rock, creating sediment.

Magma shoots out of a volcano as lava.

Rocks on the surface.

Igneous rock forms.

Sediment moves around then deposits, or settles.

Magma cools.

Sediment is squeezed together.

Magma

Sedimentary rock forms.

Rocks melt into magma.

High temperature and pressure change the forms of rocks.

Metamorphic rock forms.

Look at the diagram above. Start with the label "Igneous rock forms." Then follow the arrows to see how one type of rock can be turned into another type.

Lava typically flows very slowly—at 0.6 miles (1 kilometer) per hour.

A volcanologist takes lava samples at an active volcano in Ethiopia, Africa.

Exploring Rocks

Rocks hold the secrets to Earth and its past. They tell us how our planet formed, what it looked like millions of years ago, and how it continues to change. Scientists who study rocks are called geologists. But these scientists don't just focus on rocks! Geology is a science that deals with all of Earth's materials, structures, and processes. Geologists study the workings of our planet—and even other planets in the solar system.

Earth Detectives

Geology has many fields of study. Mineralogists study minerals to figure out the composition, age, and properties of rocks. Paleontologists study fossils to learn what life was like on Earth in the past. Volcanologists get up close to volcanoes to figure out when they might erupt. Seismologists look at Earth's structures to predict earthquakes. And planetary geologists study moons, asteroids, comets, and rocks on other planets.

Planetary geologists study how rocks in space, such as this asteroid, form and change.

Meet a Geologist

Dr. Kelsey Young works at the National Aeronautics and Space Administration (NASA). She is a field geologist!

Q. What do you do at NASA?

A. I spend a lot of time out in the field, meaning I go to places. I go to places on Earth that look like places on other planets. For example, I go to volcanoes on Earth that look like volcanoes on our moon or Mars. These are sites that tell us how surfaces on other planets form and change.

Q. What are some unexpected things that have happened to you in the field?

A. No two days are the same. I've had my share of crazy bad-weather days while camping in remote Canada, or wildlife encounters that I didn't expect, or clouds of black flies that affect the work that I'm doing. In the field, there's always an adventure!

Dr. Young working in the field

Q. What else do you do as part of your job?

A. I also help determine what astronauts will be doing when they are on our moon and Mars. I help figure out what kinds of rocks they are going to be collecting and bringing home to Earth, how they will pick them up, and what kinds of tools they will need.

Q. What are your tips for kids who might want to become geologists?

A. Spend time outside and ask questions about what you're seeing. When you're doing that, you're doing science.

Essential Tools

Field Journal: used to write down and sketch observations about rock formations, such as their location, shape, color, and size.

Rock Hammer: breaks apart rocks so the user can collect samples to study in the lab. It's important that a sample come from inside a rock, because a rock's surface has been exposed to the weather. Exposure to the weather could change chemicals in the rock and also allow bacteria to grow on the surface.

Hand Magnifier: helps geologists look closely at rocks, the minerals they contain, and even small fossils trapped inside.

Tools of the Trade

These are some of the essential tools geologists use to study rocks and minerals in the field. They then study samples in the lab using microscopes and other machines.

Global Positioning System tracker (GPS): uses satellites in orbit around Earth to track the location of objects. Geologists use GPS to record the exact location of landforms and rock formations in the field.

Ground-Penetrating Radar (GPR): sends invisible vibrations into the ground. By analyzing how those vibrations bounce back, geologists can map what's beneath their feet, including rock layers and water.

X-Ray Fluorescence Spectrometer (XFS): uses X-rays to determine the types and quantity of elements and minerals inside a rock. Geologists use this device to identify rock types within minutes.

Rocks are amazing! They are all around us and provide lots of information about Earth and our planet's history. They also help us understand how our planet functions. And as Earth continues to change, there is always more to discover!

Name That Rock!

Ready to test your rock smarts? The photos on this spread show famous rock formations around the world. Read the hint, then guess what type of rock makes up each formation from the choices below. The answers are on page 39.

Basalt   **Gneiss**   **Granite**   **Limestone**   **Marble**   **Sandstone**

1 Hint: This 46-foot (14-meter) natural rock arch is made of sand grains that were pressed together and turned into stone over time. (See page 19.)

Natural columns of Giant's Causeway formation in Northern Ireland

Delicate Arch at Arches National Park in Utah

2 Hint: These rocks formed when lava spewed out of volcanoes between 60 and 55 million years ago. (See page 17.)

El Capitan at Yosemite National Park in California

3 Hint: This 3,000-foot (914-m) rock wall is made of coarse rock that formed when magma cooled deep underground. (See page 16.)

4 Hint: These caves are made of a type of rock that was transformed deep underground from limestone. (See page 21.)

Cave walls by the sea in Patagonia, Chile

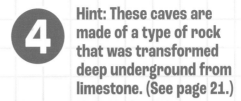

The Dolomites mountain range in Italy

5 Hint: This mountain range is made of rock that was a coral reef about 250 million years ago. (See page 19.)

6 Hint: This 3.8-billion-year-old gray and white rock formation is made of a type of rock that was transformed deep underground from either granite or sedimentary rock. (See page 21.)

Amîtsoq formation in Greenland

ANSWERS: 1. Sandstone; 2. Basalt; 3. Granite; 4. Marble; 5. Limestone; 6. Gneiss

Surface Rocks

One of the first things geologists do when exploring a new site is determine the types of rocks found at the surface. They record this information on geologic maps. The map on page 41 shows the types of surface rocks that make up the continental United States. Study the map, then answer the questions below.

Analyze It!

1 What is the most common type of surface rock?

2 Where are most igneous rocks found?

3 What trends, or patterns, do you see on the map?

4 How many states contain metamorphic rock?

The answers are on page 41.

Surface Rocks of the Continental United States

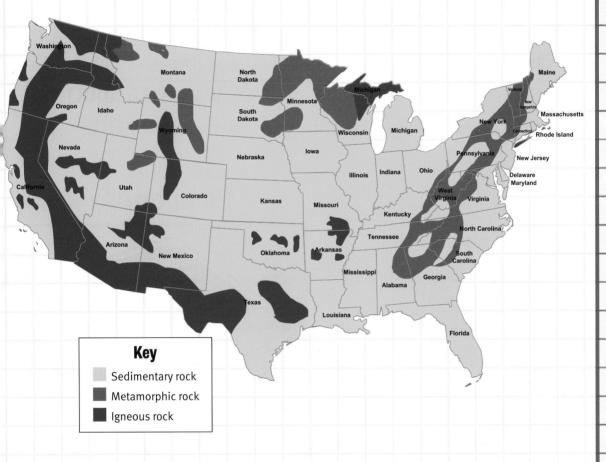

Key

- Sedimentary rock
- Metamorphic rock
- Igneous rock

ANSWERS: 1. Sedimentary; 2. The surface rocks in the central part of the United States; 3. The western part of the United States. Igneous rocks are mostly in the western part, and metamorphic rocks are mostly in the eastern part; 4. 27.

Erosion in Action!

Wind, water, and gravity erode rocks over time. During this activity, you can witness how these forces of nature wear away and move sediments. **YOU WILL NEED ADULT SUPERVISION FOR STEP THREE OF THIS EXPERIMENT.**

Materials

Book (about 2 in [5 cm] thick)

Baking pan

Soil

Small rocks

Bowl

Bottle of water

Paper

Pencil

Hair dryer

Directions

1. Prop the book under one end of the baking pan. Mix the soil and small rocks together in the bowl. Pack the mixture on the pan's raised end to create a slope that stops halfway down the pan.

2 Slowly pour the water down the slope. This mimics rainwater or a river flowing on the surface. What happens to the soil? What about the small rocks? Record your observations on a piece of paper.

3 <u>With help from a trusted adult</u>, use the hair dryer to blow air over the slope. This mimics the wind. How does the wind affect the soil and the rocks? Keep recording your observations.

4 Repeat steps 2 and 3 several times. What happens to the sediments over time? Where do the sediments end up? Record how your slope looks after erosion by wind and water.

Explain It!

Using what you learned in this book, can you explain what happened and why? If you need help, turn back to pages 26–27.

True Statistics

Earth's age: About 4.6 billion years old

Age of oldest known rocks on Earth (found in Australia): 4 billion years old

Thickness of Earth's crust under the continents: Between 12 and 43 miles (20 and 70 km)

Thickness of Earth's crust under the oceans: Between 3 and 6 miles (5 and 10 km)

Length of the deepest hole dug into Earth's crust by scientists: 7.5 miles (12 km)

Estimated number of natural stone arches at Arches National Park in Utah: 2,000

Maximum eruption temperature of magma: 2192°F (1200°C)

Height of the world's largest sandstone rock (found in Australia): 1,141 feet 8 inches (348 m)

Did you find the truth?

F The oldest rocks on Earth are 10 billion years old.

T Earth's crust is made up of the continents and ocean floor.

Resources

Other books in this series:

 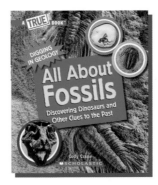 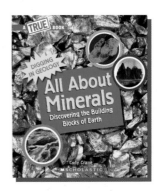

You can also look at:

Fretland VanVoorst, Jennifer. *Igneous Rocks*. New York: Scholastic, 2020.

Fretland VanVoorst, Jennifer. *Metamorphic Rocks*. New York: Scholastic, 2020.

Fretland VanVoorst, Jennifer. *Sedimentary Rocks*. New York: Scholastic, 2020.

Green, Dan, and the Smithsonian Institution. *The Rock and Gem Book . . . And Other Treasures of the Natural World*. New York: DK Publishing, 2016.

Woolf, Alex. *The Science of Rocks and Minerals: The Hard Truth About the Stuff Beneath Our Feet*. New York: Scholastic, 2018.

Glossary

deposition (deh-poh-ZISH-uhn): the addition of material to a landform, creating a new landform such as an island

electrocution (i-lek-truh-KYOO-shn): death or injury caused by severe electric shock

elements (EL-eh-ments): substances that cannot be broken down into simpler substances

erosion (i-ROH-zhuhn): the wearing away by wind or water

gravity (GRAV-i-tee): the force that pulls objects toward the center of Earth and keeps them from floating away

igneous (IG-nee-uhs): rocks that are produced by great heat or by a volcano

metamorphic (met-uh-MOR-fik): rocks whose structure has been changed by pressure, heat, or fluids, making them a different type of rock

minerals (MIN-ur-uhls): solid, natural substances that do not come from an animal or a plant

sedimentary (sed-eh-MEN-tur-ee): rocks that formed from layers of materials that have been pressed together

tectonic plates (tek-TAH-nik playts): huge slabs of rock that make up Earth's outer layer (Earth's lithosphere—the crust and uppermost mantle) and move very slowly

weathering (WETH-ur-ing): the breaking apart of rocks over time due to water, wind, and gravity

Index

Page numbers in **bold** indicate illustrations.

About the Author

Alessandra Potenza is a science journalist based in New York. She studied journalism at Columbia University and is currently the senior editor of Scholastic's *SuperScience* magazine. Alessandra is originally from Rome, Italy. She loves reading books, traveling, stargazing, and geeking out about science. Please visit her website at www.alepotenza.com.